A Gullah Alphabet

Margie Willis Clary

illustrated by Dennis L. Brown

SANDLAPPER PUBLISHING CO., INC.
ORANGEBURG, SOUTH CAROLINA USA

FIRST EDITION

Published by Sandlapper Publishing Co., Inc.
  1281 Amelia Street
  Orangeburg, SC 29115
  www.sandlapperpublishing.com

Manufactured in Korea

Library of Congress Cataloging-in-Publication Data

Clary, Margie Willis, 1931–
    A Gullah alphabet / Margie Wilis Clary ; illustrated by Dennis
  L. Brown. — 1st ed.
          p. cm.
    Includes bibliographical references.
    ISBN-13: 978-0-87844-184-6 (hardcover : alk. paper)
    ISBN-10: 0-87844-184-0 (hardcover : alk. paper)
  1. Sea Islands Creole dialect—Alphabet—Juvenile literature.   I.
Brown, Dennis L. II. Title

PM7875.G8C57 2007
427'.975799—dc22
                                    2007032237

છી

Dedicated to
the memory of
JOE HAROLD MIDDLETON
Gullah Storyteller
1931–2007

જી

A *Gullah Alphabet* is dedicated to my late father, Joe H. Middleton, a storyteller. When asked by the author to contribute a word about my father for this book, I felt honored.

Dad lived most of his life in southeastern South Carolina and, knowing his love for the area and its inhabitants, he would have been proud to be associated with this project. He had a passion for preserving the tradition of, not only the Gullah dialect, but storytelling, as well, and worked to keep both alive for future generations. Through his storytelling, he passed to us Gullah tales told to him by others throughout his life. These stories, and Dad's artful delivery of them, touched many people. That is the mission of a storyteller.

I like to think this book is dedicated not only to my father but to all storytellers. That's the way *Missah Joe* would have wanted it. Enjoy the book and **pass it on**!

Todd Middleton
Pawley's Island, South Carolina

INTRODUCTION

It is said that the Gullah language originated around 1700 among the Africans who were brought to America to work. They came from the continent's rice-growing region on the West Coast, countries we now know as Senegal, Sierra Leone, Guinea-Bissau, Guinea, and Liberia. With the rise in demand for rice grown on the southern plantations, it was important to look for laborers skilled in rice production. It was the skill of these Gullah farmers that made rice one of the most successful industries in the colony of Carolina.

A second group of Africans came through the ports of Charleston and Savannah from Angola in southern Africa. Others came from Ghana and the West Indies. It is believed by some that the word "Gullah" was derived from "Gola," the Africans' pronunciation of Angola.

Coming from over two dozen ethic backgrounds, all speaking different languages, it was difficult for the Africans to communicate with one another. Out of necessity, they had to develop a means of communication. Their first efforts produced what is called pidgin English. During the following generation they formed a Creole language called Gullah. Gullah refers to the spoken language. Verbs have no tense. Pronouns have no gender. "That's he book" can refer to a girl's or a boy's book.

As Gullah has, over the generations, been a spoken language, preserving this beautiful and melodious speech in writing has been difficult. The American Bible Society made a notable effort with the translation of the Gospel of Luke into contemporary Gullah. Before her death in 1994, South Carolina Gullah storyteller Tita Heins was assisting Wycliffe Publishers in translating the Bible. De Nyew Testament was published in 2005. Virginia Mixson Geraty of Yonges Island, near Charleston, did much research into the Gullah language before her death in 2006. In 1997, she published Gulluh Fuh Oonuh (Gullah for You), A Guide to the Gullah Language [Sandlapper Publishing Co., Inc.]. Joe Harold Middleton, a well-known Gullah storyteller and a personal friend, made Gullah come alive to all who knew him. His knowledge and presentation of the language through the telling of stories brought enjoyment to all ages. It was Joe who inspired me to pen this book. We were collaborating on the Gullah alphabet translation when he died in February of this year.

A Gullah Alphabet is written to introduce children to the beauty of the Gullah language. My hope is, it will encourage further research and study of the language and culture.

A taste often leads to a bigger helping!

A iz fa **Affiky**, de Gullah foke netib soil.

A is for **Africa**, the Gullah folks' native soil.

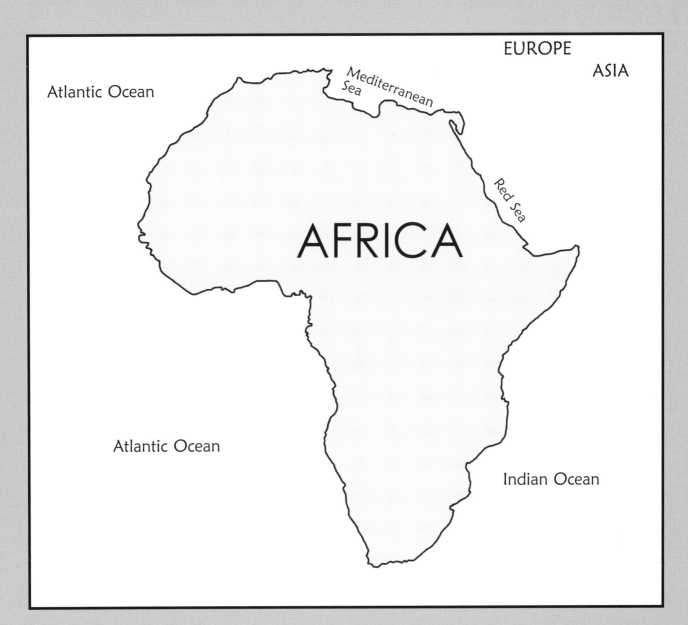

B iz fa de **buckra** dat mek we fa toil.

B is for the **white man** that brought them here to toil.

C iz fa de **chillun**, ney Mudda fut dey play.

C is for the **children**, at Mama's feet they play.

D

D iz fa **dayclean**, de fus lite uh dey.

D is for **dawn**, the first light of day.

E iz fa de **eart** weh dem sow de yam.

E is for the **earth** where to plant the yams.

F iz fa **fush** dem ketch—cat, swimp, en clam.

F is for **fish** they caught—cat, shrimp, and clam.

G iz fa de **grabe** ya ley en heaven boun.

G is for the **grave** where you lay when heaven bound.

H iz fa de **haabis** wen de crop git gedda roun.

H is for the **harvest** when crops are gathered in.

I

I iz fa de **indigo** de buckra git frum de lan.

I is for the **indigo** the white man planted on the land.

J iz fa de **jeybud** dat da chatta ney de han.

J is for the **jay bird** that chatters close at hand.

K iz fa de **kubba** dat heat de col knee.

K is the **cover** that warms your freezing knees.

L iz fa de **leabes** tunnin culla puntop de tree.

L is for the **leaves** turning colors on the trees.

M iz fa de **Missee** she da sho off en de big house.

M is for the **Mistress** who entertains in the big house.

N iz fa de **Nited State ub Merika**, de Gullah foke udda home.

N is for the **United States of America**, the Gullah folks' adopted home.

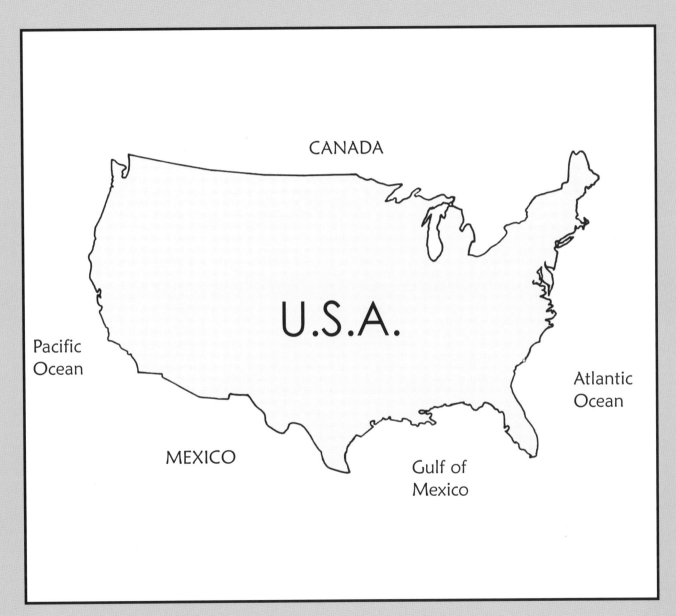

O

O iz fa de **oomen**, en fa de **ok'a** gumba he da cook.

O is for the **woman** and for the **okra** gumbo she cooks.

P iz fa de **peacha** dat taak frum de Holy Book.

P is for the **preacher** that preaches from the Bible.

Q iz fa de **quilt** dem put tagedda en de quilting be.

Q is for the **quilt** made at a quilting bee.

R iz fa de **rice** dat grow ney de sea.

R is for the **rice** that grew near the sea.

S iz fa ma **sistah** dat cum fa see we.

S is for my **sister** that comes to visit me.

T

T iz fa de **taripen** dem call'um cutta be.

T is for the **terrapin**, sometimes called a cooter.

U iz fa **um**, ma brodda him be.

U is for **him**, my brother.

V iz fa de **vamint** en de daak we see.

V is for **varmints** that at night you see.

W iz fa de **wagin** dat tote de hebby lode.

W is for the **wagon** that carries the heavy loads.

Y iz fa de **yaad** him brush frum de hous ta
de road.

Y is for the **yard** she sweeps from the
house to the road.

BIBLIOGRAPHY

Baird, Keith E., and Twining. *Sea Island Roots*. Trenton: Africa World Press, Inc., 1991.

Botkin, B. A. *A Treasury of Southern Folklore*. New York: American Legacy, Press, 1977.

———. *A Treasury of American Folklore*. New York: American Legacy Press, 1989.

Carawan, Guy, and Candie Carawan, eds. *Ain't you got a right to the tree of life?* Athens: University of Georgia Press, 1986.

Daise, Ronald. *Little Muddy Waters*. Beaufort, SC: G.O.G. Enterprise, 1997.

———. *Reminiscences of Sea Island Heritage*. Orangeburg, SC: Sandlapper Publishing, 1986.

Edgar, Walter. *South Carolina, A History*. Columbia, SC: University of South Carolina Press, 1998.

Frasier, Eugene. *James Island*. Charleston, SC: South Carolina History Press, 2006.

Faseyin, Awotunde. *The Gullah Retrospect*. 2004. http://newafrikanvodun.com/gullah.html.

Geraty, Virginia Mixson. *Gulluh Fuh Oonuh (Gullah For You)*. Orangeburg, SC: Sandlapper Publishing Co., Inc., 1997.

Gonzales, Ambrose E. *The Black Border*. Columbia, SC: The State Company, 1922.

Harris, Joel Chandler. *Uncle Remus*. New York: Grosset & Dunlap Publishers, 1921.

Jackson, Patricia Jones. *When Roots Die*. Athens, GA: University of Georgia Press, 1987.

Mitchell, Allen. *Wadmalaw Island, Leaving Traditional Roots Behind*. Roslyn, PA: Boar Hog Tree Press, 1996.

Pollitzer, William S. *The Gullah People and Their African Heritage*. Athens, GA: University of Georgia Press, 1999.

Rhyne, Nancy. *Chronicles of the South Carolina Sea Islands*. Winston-Salem: John F. Blair, 1998.

———. *Touring the Coastal South Carolina Backroads*. Winston-Salem: John F. Blair, 1992.

Turner, Lorenzo Dow. *Africanisms in the Gullah Dialect*. Columbia, SC: University of South Carolina Press, 2002.

About the Author:
MARGIE WILLIS CLARY is a retired elementary school teacher, a professional storyteller, and a published author. She holds a masters in education. Clary is actively involved with the National Association of Storytellers, The International Reading Association, The Society of Children's Book Writers and Illustrators, and state and local arts councils. Her other books include *Searching the Lights, Spirits & Legends, Make It Three: The Story of the CSS H. L. Hunley*, and *A Sweet, Sweet Basket*. Clary lives in Charleston with her husband Ralph.

• Margie Clary can be contacted by email at mwclary@juno.com.

About the Illustrator:
DENNIS LEE BROWN is a self-taught painter. He grew up in South Carolina and lives in Charleston. This is the second project on which he has collaborated with Margie Clary. His beautiful pastels in *A Sweet, Sweet Basket* bring the art and tradition of sweetgrass basketweaving to life. In *A Gullah Alphabet*, Brown's connection with the Lowcountry and the Gullah people who inhabit the islands is obvious.

• For information on his artwork and availability, Dennis Brown can be contacted by phone at 843-270-8157 and by email at dlbrown04@knology.net.

OTHER BOOKS FOR YOUNG READERS BY MARGIE WILLIS CLARY

A Sweet, Sweet Basket
illustrated by Dennis L. Brown
ISBN 978-0-87844-127-3
hardcover
$16.95

A Teaching Guide to A Sweet, Sweet Basket
saddle stitch
$9.95

Searching the Lights
illustrated by Valerie J. Luedtke
ISBN 978-0-87844-138-9
hardcover
$16.95

Make It Three: The Story of the CSS H. L. Hunley Civil War Submarine
with illustrations by Becky Rickenbaker
ISBN 978-0-87844-158-7
paperback
$9.95

Spirits & Legends
ISBN 978-0-9669707-1-5
paperback
$12.95